SPEND Your Way to Wealth

Seven Common Sense Steps to Black Prosperity

Author : Bonhomme, Jean
ISBN : 978-1-7350060-0-0

National Black Men's Health Network

Dedication

This book is dedicated to Black people (and especially Black families) who are working their fingers to the bone all the time, but who feel like they just can't get ahead.

Hopefully, this book will point them to a better way.

Acknowledgements

This book would not have been possible without the support and encouragement of Chike Acua, Delxino Wilson DeBriano, Quy-Yuim "Baba Bey" the African Godfather, Juanita Cato, Mona Scott and others too numerous to mention.

INTRODUCTION

CAUTION: Businesses set up by people outside the Black community may not want Black people to read this. They want you to unknowingly keep Black dollars benefitting only them.

There are powerful choices that the Black community in America was never taught to make that can create wealth and overcome poverty. Overall, Black Americans have clearly lower incomes and higher poverty rates than whites, as well as lagging behind many other ethnic groups.

Most people think Black economic problems come from issues like lower wages, higher unemployment rates, lower literacy levels and higher incarceration rates. While it is entirely true that these harsh realities don't do Black people any good, there is a major reason that is completely within our control, that has a huge impact on Black people's chances of accumulating wealth and escaping poverty:

It is the spending choices of Black people.

There are immigrants who come to this country with no money, not able to even speak English, who turn up wealthy twenty years later. Some even own chains of successful businesses and the like. On the other hand, there are many people who come into huge sums of money (such as lottery winners) who are heavily in debt ten years later. **The issue was never how much money they started with, but how they spent however much or little money they had.**

Blacks living in the U.S. that come from the West Indies tend to have higher than average incomes compared to people in the U.S. overall. Why? Because having lived in Black nations, West Indians usually have some grasp of commerce and money management. This proves that there is nothing inherent to being Black that dooms the Black community to poverty. What we need to find out is "what do more successful communities know that most of us don't?"

This book explains exactly that. The author firmly believes in the KISS principle: Keep It Short and Sweet. Clear, direct talk seasoned with instructive pictures will help you to a better understanding of how Black dollars can be used to build up our own communities, not only in the future but often with immediate benefits.

KNOWLEDGE IS POWER.

NOW HELP YOURSELF TO SOME.

I Black Poverty: The REAL Cause We Don't Talk About.

A deeply religious man asked God to show him Heaven and Hell. God shows him hell first. He sees an ugly place where people looked terrible, like living skeletons, mouths dry and cracked. In the center of hell was a bottomless pit. In the center of the pit was a huge pot of the most delicious smelling stew you could ever imagine. However, the only way to reach the stew was by spoons with very long handles

Every time one of the dwellers of hell would scoop out some of the stew and try to turn it around to feed their own mouth, all the stew would spill out of the spoon into the pit and be lost.

FOOD SPILLING INTO THE PIT

The man was visibly shaken. He said, "my God, my God, what a terrible fate. To be eternally suffering from intense hunger and thirst but unable to die, all in the midst of plenty, with that incredibly tantalizing smell. Who could imagine a worse fate? Please, God, this is too much for me. Please show me Heaven

He was instantly transported to a place where people were all well-fed, serene, appearing very happy, and at total peace. But he noted that in the center of Heaven was a bottomless pit over which was suspended a pot of the same delicious smelling stew with long handled spoons, exactly the same set-up as he had seen in Hell.

He said, "God, I don't understand this at all. Both Heaven and Hell are set up identically, what is the difference?"

God replied:

"It's very simple. These are the people who have learned to feed each other."

The Black community could be economic heaven. The annual income of Black America reached an estimated total earned income of $836 billion in 2011. This is greater than the gross national product of many nations. In fact, news commentator Larry Elder stated that if Black America were a country, it would be the 15th wealthiest in the world. There are over two million Black businesses in the U.S. Yet, the Black community looks more like economic hell, for exactly the same reason: ***we have not learned to feed each other.***

The real problem? The Black community is one of the few places where most of the money that enters goes right back out just as soon as it comes in, going to businesses owned by whites, Asians, megastore chains and the like.

This is not putting down people of other races, ethnicities, or religions. It is just pointing out something we need to learn.

Black people are functionally poor mainly because our spending is not directed at feeding each other.

When you spend with a person from your own community, you support their income.

When a person from your community spends with you, they support your income.

When each of us spends outside our community, we fail to support incomes within our community.

Other groups BUY from each other but SELL to us!

How Black people became so poor becomes a chicken or the egg question.

Are Black people poor just because of low income, or do we have low incomes mostly because our misdirected spending?

The answer is simple: one couldn't happen without the other.

If we bought from each other, we would be supporting each other's incomes

The solution:

Black People can redirect our spending!

II. Let's look at a little example of how we do things in the Black community:

Seated: a Black realtor, a Black car salesman, a Black insurance agent, and a Black grocer. Each has a billfold of money in their hands.

Realtor

Car Salesman

Insurance Agent

Grocer

The realtor needs a car. She gets up and leaves her seat to go shopping outside her community. **She comes back to her seat with car keys, but no money.**

**THE REALTOR NOW HAS CAR KEYS,
BUT NO MORE MONEY TO SPEND**

The insurance agent needs a home. He gets up and leaves his seat to go shopping outside his community. **He comes back to his seat with house keys, but no money.**

THE INSURANCE AGENT NOW HAS A HOUSE, BUT NO MORE MONEY TO SPEND

The car salesman needs groceries. He gets up and leaves his seat to go shopping outside his community. **He comes back to his seat with a grocery bag, but no money.**

THE CAR SALESMAN NOW HAS GROCERIES, BUT NO MORE MONEY TO SPEND

The grocer needs insurance. She gets up and leaves her seat to go shopping outside her community. **She comes back to her seat with a policy, but no money.**

THE GROCER NOW HAS A POLICY, BUT NO MORE MONEY TO SPEND

What happened?

All the money that came into the Black community went right back out of it with a single purchase.

Now for any of these people to buy anything else they need; they need do more work to bring in more money!

III. Now let's try this a different way:

The Black Realtor needs a car. She gets up and leaves her seat to go shopping from the Black car salesman sitting across from her. She comes back to her seat with car keys, **but the car salesman now has two billfolds.**

THE REALTOR HAS HER CAR KEYS.

THE CAR SALESMAN NOW HAS EXTRA MONEY

Black Car Salesman Contacts				
Contact's Name	**Business Name Email Address Website**	**Phone #**	**When will you contact business owner?**	**Completed business with them?**
Notes:				

The car salesman needs a home. He gets up and leaves his seat to go shopping, this **time from the Black realtor** sitting across from him. He comes back to his seat with house keys, and **the realtor now has a set of car keys and a billfold again.**

THE REALTOR NOW HAS A CAR *AND* MONEY!

Black Realtors/Real Estate Agents				
Contact's Name	**Business Name Email Address Website**	**Phone #**	**When will you contact business owner?**	**Completed business with them?**

Notes:

THE CAR SALESMAN NOW HAS A HOUSE *AND* MONEY!

The insurance agent needs groceries. He gets up and leaves his seat to go shopping, this time from the Black grocer sitting across from him. He comes back to his seat with a grocery bag, but **the grocer now has two billfolds.**

THE INSURANCE AGENT NOW HAS GROCERIES.

THE GROCER NOW HAS TWO BILLFOLDS

Black Insurance Agents				
Contact's Name	**Business Name Email Address Website**	**Phone #**	**When will you contact business owner?**	**Completed business with them?**
Notes:				

The grocer needs insurance. She gets up and leaves her seat to go shopping from the insurance agent sitting across from her. She comes back to her seat with a policy, but **she still has a billfold left and now the insurance agent has a billfold again along WITH his house.**

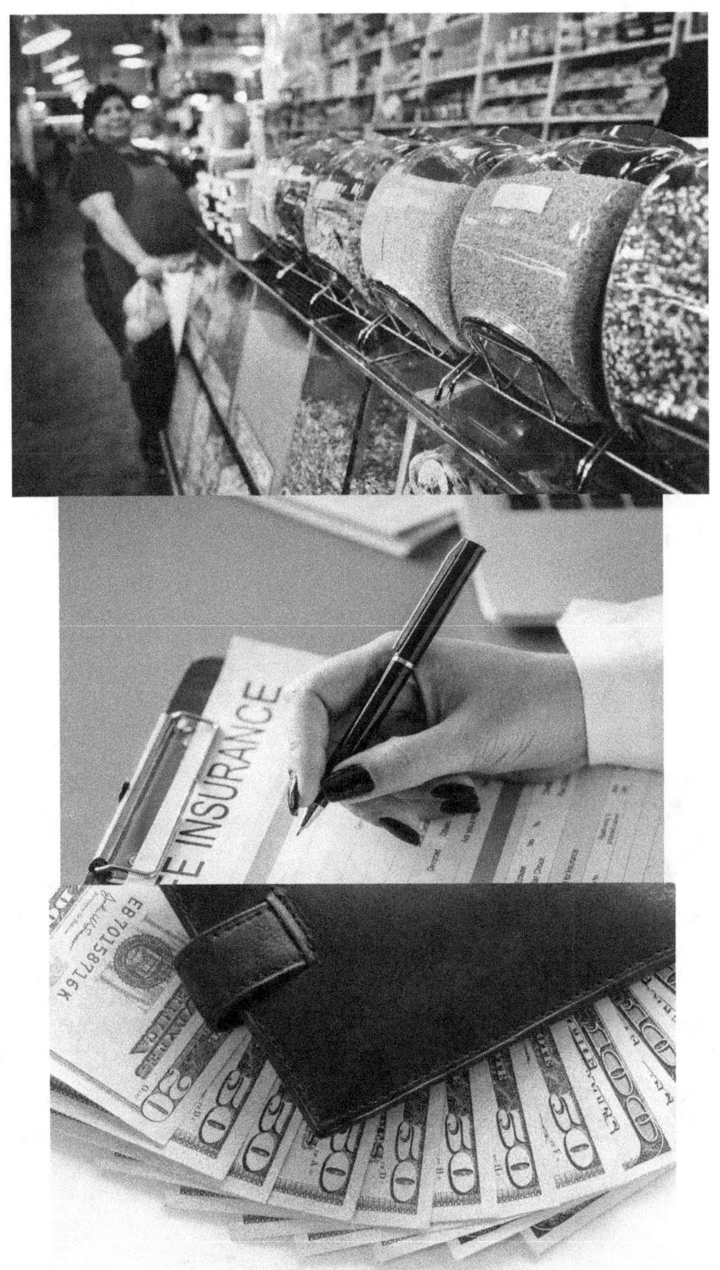

THE GROCER NOW HAS A POLICY *AND* MONEY!

INSURANCE AGENT NOW HAS A HOUSE *AND* MONEY!

Black Grocers				
Contact's Name	**Business Name Email Address Website**	**Phone #**	**When will you contact business owner?**	**Completed business with them?**
Notes:				

IT'S NOT ALWAYS ABOUT *HOW MUCH* MONEY YOU HAVE, BUT *WHERE* YOU SPEND IT!

Do you see what happened here?

Now they all have the goods they wanted, but they all still have money also,

They can continue purchasing almost endlessly, as long as they keep buying from each other.

Now the Black realtor can also buy insurance for the car from the Black insurance agent, the Black insurance agent can buy a car from the Black car salesman, the Black car salesmen can buy groceries from the Black grocer, and the Black grocer can buy a home from the Black realtor.

By buying and trading from each other, they can go on and on until they all have everything they need, and still have money left at the end to continue buying.

Black Business Contacts				
Contact's Name	**Business Name Email Address Website**	**Phone #**	**When will you contact business owner?**	**Completed business with them?**
Notes:				

Do you see how this all fits into the parable of heaven and hell? Do you see how the exact same setup can result in disastrous results or wonderful results depending on whether or not we take care of each other?

In case you are wondering where this story, called **the parable of the long spoons**, came from, it is of Hebrew origin. This is how Jews as such a small minority amass such great wealth. The Jewish doctor uses the Jewish banker, who uses the Jewish lawyer, who uses the Jewish realtor, who uses they Jewish car salesman, and so forth. It is estimated that any money that enters the Jewish community changes hands inside that community an average of seven times before it leaves. This does not just apply to Jews either. **This is not criticizing Jews, just saying that we should start doing do what they do.** Asians, Indians, other ethnicities, and mega-chains set up businesses in Black communities hoping to do the exact same thing. While **they focus on BUYING from each other they focus on SELLING to us. That way their money stays theirs while they keep adding OUR money to theirs**.

Other ethnicities have been known to call black people "liquid money." That's because when you try to pick up water, it seeps right out between your fingers. That's just how money behaves in most Black people's hands. Blacks often work themselves sick to bring in money, but it all flows right away into the hands of people who aren't black. This is a well-known and great business opportunity for people of other groups. We'll take our paychecks and tax refunds straight to the Asian nail salon, the Indian convenience store and the white owned megastore chains.

Not only is our own money flowing right out of our hands like water, we are often buying products that we ourselves built and others are the only ones getting the profit. An African proverb says, "**it's a fool whose own tomatoes are sold to him.**"

This is not to put down other ethnic groups, but to show us what we are doing wrong and how it hurts us. The only way to counter this is to learn to keep the money in black hands, and that has to mean buying in our own communities. **Other ethnicities keep their money to themselves. The single greatest economic advance black people could make is to learn to do the same thing for ourselves.**

Most white money stays in white hands. Why can't we do the same?

IV. Here is a big surprise for many of you: There is a big difference between wealth and income.

Income is **what you bring in**, while wealth is **what you accumulate**. Most of us think that if we get our hands on a lot of money, all poverty will be over. Think though, how many of us have come into a sizeable amount of money and watched it disappear so fast we didn't have time to figure out what happened? There is nothing wrong with obtaining a lot of money, but how you spend it is critical to whether it will be maintained, replenished, increase or vanish quickly.

Compare that with the situation of some immigrants, many of who came into the United States unable to even speak the English language. Twenty years later, many of them are multi-millionaires, owning chains of restaurants, dry cleaners, etc. Did they work very hard? Did they put in long hours? Almost certainly, that's how they got it. But the reason they **kept** it is another story. They supported their communities and their communities supported them. You can go by certain parts of town and see whole businesses dominated by a certain ethnicity, such as Indians owning motels, Asians owning beauty stores, and even entire strip malls representing a single ethnicity.

Think all NFL players are set for life? One out of six NFL players files for bankruptcy within twelve years of retirement.

Retired NFL Players Going Bankrupt

The NBER study is based on data from all NFL players drafted from 1996 to 2003.

Within 12 years of retirement	Likelihood of bankruptcy**
15.7%	**3x**
of NFL players go bankrupt* (one out of six)	greater for NFL players compared to general population

*The 15.7% only focuses on bankruptcy rates and actual filings in bankruptcy court. However, there are many athletes experiencing financial distress who are not captured in this study and statistic since they did not declare bankruptcy in federal court.
**The likelihood of bankruptcy is based on annual hazard rates, which measure the probability of going bankrupt in a given period of time.

Seven out of ten lottery winners are in debt seven years after winning tens or even hundreds of millions of dollars. One major pitfall is spending money on things that don't last, like cars, clothes and parties.

There is an old saying – "guns, not butter," which means buy enduring goods, not things that only last a short while. If you don't accumulate anything, you will never be wealthy no matter how much you earn.

These two great champions had a lot but lost a lot.

Mike Tyson earned $3-400 million over his boxing career. That's more than 100 average black families will make over their lifetimes, but it is all gone now.

Holyfield's mansion was recently foreclosed.

That only goes to show you, income is what you make, but only wealth is what you get to keep.

V. The Sensible Steps:

Step Number One:
Focus on Buying IN and FROM the Black Community.
Always aim to keep your money in the family!

These two look like they KEPT their money in the family.

Step Number Two:
It's OK to sell within your own community, but whenever possible, this is even BETTER. When dealing with other communities, focus on SELLING. Bring THEIR dollars over to us. You may say other groups won't buy from blacks, but with avenues like internet sales, no one knows who they are buying from.

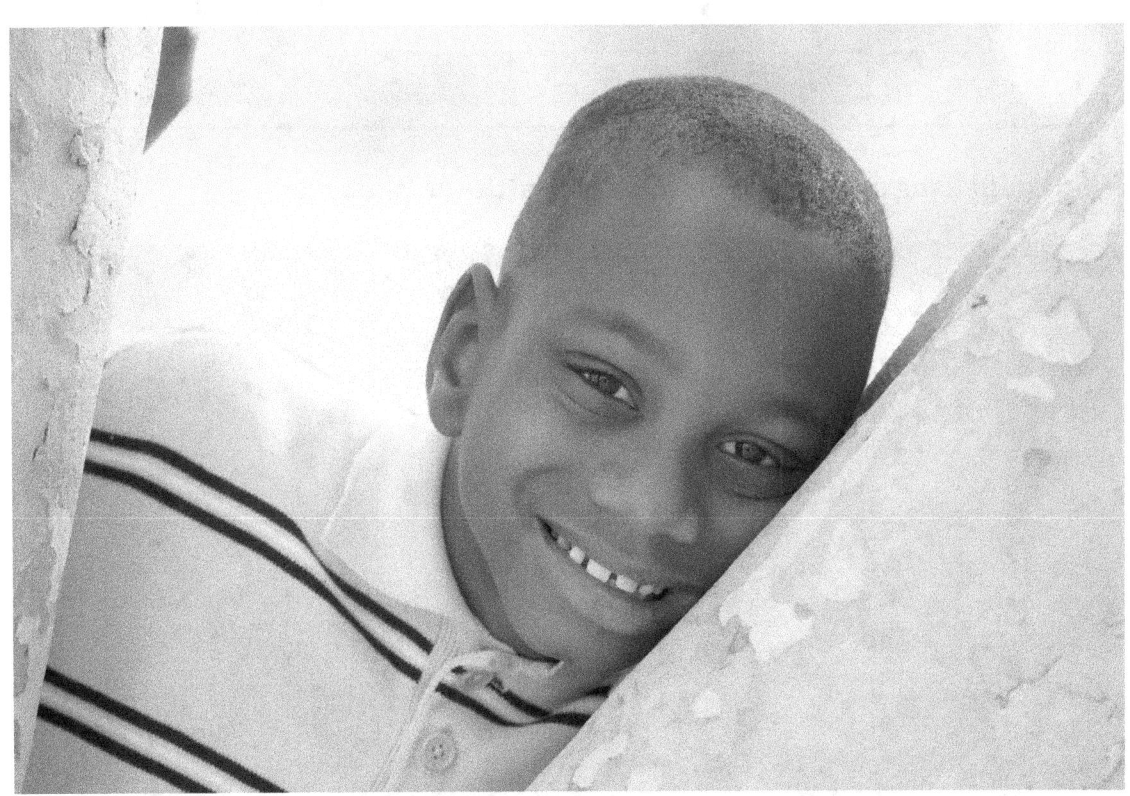

Step Number Three:
Buy things that will hold and increase their value over time, such as real estate, well-chosen stocks and precious metals.

Here's an interesting bumper sticker:

Who could hang on to any money with an attitude like that?

Step Number Four:
Avoid putting too much money into things with rapidly decreasing value over time like clothes, cars, cigarettes, alcohol, partying, etc.

This is what someone feels like when they didn't waste their money.

The Biggest Problem:
Why are Blacks so reluctant to buy Black?

You may think that Blacks buying Black just isn't going to happen. Too many of us have had bad experiences dealing with black owned businesses. Blacks have a reputation, sadly often deserved, of giving poor service, late service, failing to provide agreed upon paid for service, or not being able to offer services at a competitive price. Even those who already understand that buying Black is vitally important have felt forced to do otherwise due to a long and disappointing history.

Let's rethink that: **what if there was a business devoted to screening Black providers to make sure that they offered high quality and good pricing?** What if there was a group that would not accept Black providers that fail to deliver on their promises and do so in a timely and cost-effective fashion? **Newsflash: it IS happening, right here and now, with the Black Business Network.** You may think that Black products and services can't compete, but not with these folks.

They screen out those who can't or won't deliver. Capable Black professionals are building a community of mutually supportive buyers and sellers, a community that you can be part of.

You may say," Well, I'm not a business owner. I don't market or sell a product or service. How can any of this benefit me?" The answer is that when Black businesses prosper, Black job opportunities grow. Successful businesses need workers of all kinds to make and sell their services and products. Even if you are not in business yourself, the entire community prospers from a greatly expanded job market. Not only that, well-supported Black businesses have the financial resources to offer better prices and services that can compete with anything the megastores can offer.

Step Number Five:
If you are a business, whenever possible, buy in quantity. One of the things that more successful businesses do is buying in groups. For instance, if a black shoe retailer joins with a dozen other black shoe retailers to buy shoes, they can offer lower prices to their customers. Bigger discounts from suppliers are possible when you buy in bulk.

Step Number Six:
Focus on accumulation of assets at least as much as you focus on income.

Real wealth is what you accumulate, not how much you bring in. If you can't keep anything, you will never be wealthy no matter how much you earn.

Step Number Seven:
Research and identify reputable and effective businesses in the Black Community. Check out the Black Business Network at https://www.buyblackmovement.com/BBN/index.cfm

The Black Business Network is a ready-made resource for identifying and networking capable Black businesses and their customers. The Black Business Network is your number one resource for building a path to real and lasting wealth in the Black community.

Think about it..................

Knowledge gives us real power to shape our future. We can't depend on the government (no matter which party or politician is in power), the lottery, or anything else to change things for us. **WE need to make the choice.** Will Blacks be like the people in hell, starving in the midst of plenty, or will we create an economic heaven for ourselves by learning to feed each other?

Hell

Heaven

Which will **YOU** choose?

Hell or Heaven?

Black poverty or Black prosperity?

More and more of us are choosing to go for **economic heaven**.

Don't be left behind…………………………………………..

Black Business Contacts				
Contact's Name	**Business Name Email Address Website**	**Phone #**	**When will you contact business owner?**	**Completed business with them?**
Notes:				

FAIR USE NOTICE

About the Author

Jean Bonhomme MD. is a licensed physician who has held board certifications in Public Health, General Preventive Medicine, and Addiction Medicine. He is co-founder and president of the National Black Men's Health Network.

References:

Heaven and Hell images used by permission of Alfonso Apicella from "la campaña de Caritas Internationalis "Una sola familia humana, alimentos para todos". (The campaign of Caritas International "Only one human family, food for all.") apicella@caritas.va

Photo Credits:

Free photo 113416769 © creativecommonsstockphotos - Dreamstime.com

Free photo 6499987 © Yanik Chauvin - Dreamstime.com

Free photo 348191 © Bobby Deal - Dreamstime.com

Free photo 7721764 © Feverpitched - Dreamstime.com

Free photo 3282618 © Mary Katherine Wynn - Dreamstime.com

Free photo 4677771 © Felix Mizioznikov - Dreamstime.com

Free photo 8010878 © Laurin Rinder - Dreamstime.com

Free photo 1015582 © Laurin Rinder - Dreamstime.com

Free photo 113416769 © creativecommonsstockphotos - Dreamstime.com

www.ingramcontent.com/pod-product-compliance
Lightning Source LLC
LaVergne TN
LVHW081254100826
845148LV00009B/1222

* 9 7 8 1 7 3 5 0 0 6 0 0 0 *